Angels of the Bible

christian art kids

© 2017 Christian Art Kids,
an imprint of Christian Art Publishers,
PO Box 1599, Vereeniging, 1930, RSA

359 Longview Drive, Bloomingdale, IL, 60108, USA

First edition 2017

Cover designed by Christian Art Kids

Illustrations by Catherine Groenewald

Printed in China

ISBN 978-1-4321-1683-5

17 18 19 20 21 22 23 24 25 26 – 10 9 8 7 6 5 4 3 2 1

To:
Oceana!   Aug '19

♡ From
    " Ouma "
        Christa
                  x ♡ x

Dedicated to
my grandparents

Happy Birthday 4 This year!

Contents

Foreword

I have always been fascinated by angels. As a little girl, I always wished my mom or teacher or the librarian would give me a book filled with stories and pictures of angels.

Because I had no books to help me, I used to make real angels out of feathers for our Christmas tree. I used to daydream about what angels might look like. Mom used to tell me stories of the angel choir singing to the shepherds in the fields of Bethlehem, painting a vivid picture in my imagination.

My grandma also chipped in by teaching me that angels are everywhere at all times. I could never quite understand how they were able to walk with her between the dahlias at sunset and be wrapped up in the pages of the pile of daily devotionals resting on her nightstand. Even today, her Blue Grass perfume makes me think angels are close by.

My wish is that this book will teach young readers more about angels. I hope that it will prove what children simply know to be true and what adults find difficult to believe.

My Angels

When at night I go to sleep
sixteen angels watch over me:
Two angels guard my head
and two the edge of my bed;
two angels on my right hand
and two more on my left hand;
two angels to cover me
and two more to hover over me;
two angels show me the way
to the Lord every day;
and two angels have been given
the job of guiding me to heaven.

What Do Angels Look Like?

Although we cannot know for sure what angels really look like, the Bible does give us a few clues.

Daniel, for example, describes the angel God sent to explain a vision to him (see Daniel 10:5-6). He says that the angel was dressed in linen with a solid gold belt around his waist. His body looked like a precious stone, his face shone like lightning, his eyes looked like flaming fires, his arms and legs were like polished bronze, and his voice sounded like the roar of a big crowd.

Matthew tells us what the angel, who came to tell the women at Jesus' tomb that Jesus was alive, looked like. He says that the angel looked as bright as lightning and that his clothes were white as snow (see Matthew 28:3).

From Isaiah's description – when God showed him what heaven looks like in a dream – we also know that some angels have wings (see Isaiah 6:2).

Angels in the Bible

Throughout the Bible there are so many stories about angels - in fact they are mentioned 273 times! One of the first stories in the Bible talks about angels!

In this story, God tells Adam and Eve - the very first people God created - not to eat the fruit of the forbidden tree. When they disobey God and eat the fruit, God throws them out of the beautiful garden. To stop them from ever coming back, God orders angels to guard the entrances to the garden with flaming swords (see Genesis 3:24).

The Bible says that there are thousands and thousands of angels - too many to even count (see Revelation 5:11). Two angels are mentioned by name in the Bible. They are Gabriel and Michael.

Michael

> "At that time Michael, the archangel who stands guard over your nation, will arise." Daniel 12:1

Michael is an archangel. He is one of the strongest angels in heaven and is in charge of protecting God's people.

Michael will be the one to fight the devil and his angels in the last days. The devil was once an angel of light, but became an angel of darkness when he disobeyed God and was thrown out of heaven.

Gabriel

The angel said, "I am Gabriel! I stand in the very presence of God. It was He who sent me to bring you this good news!" Luke 1:19

Gabriel is known for being the messenger of God. The best news he ever delivered was when he told Mary that she would have a Son and that His name would be Jesus (see Luke 1:26-38).

He also told Zechariah that he would have a son named John. John would grow up to prepare the way for Jesus.

What Do Angels Do?

Angels Protect Us: Angels are heaven's soldiers. They sometimes use heavenly chariots. King David writes in the Psalms how thousands of heavenly chariots surrounded God's home (see Psalm 68:17). Imagine an entire army just to protect God's children!

Angels Protect Everything That Is Good and True: Angels know that lies are dangerous. They also know how difficult it is for us to tell the truth sometimes. The angels rejoice every time we choose to tell the truth.

Angels Are Secret Agents: Even though angels are mostly invisible, it is possible to sometimes sense when they are near. Some people say that they feel safe and happy without knowing exactly why.

Angels Are Messengers: Angels are God's messengers. In the Bible there are many stories about angels encouraging people and giving them advice.

Angels Worship God

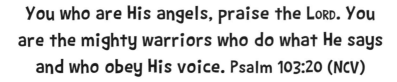

You who are His angels, praise the Lᴏʀᴅ. You are the mighty warriors who do what He says and who obey His voice. Psalm 103:20 (NCV)

Angels praise God night and day. In the last book of the Bible, it says that all of the angels gather around God's throne to worship Him: "The angels all worshiped God and said, 'Amen! Praise, glory, wisdom, thanks, honor, power, and strength belong to our God forever and ever! Amen!'" (Revelation 7:11-12, CEV).

Imagine being in the presence of all those angels worshiping God!

Let's read more about the angels in the stories that follow.

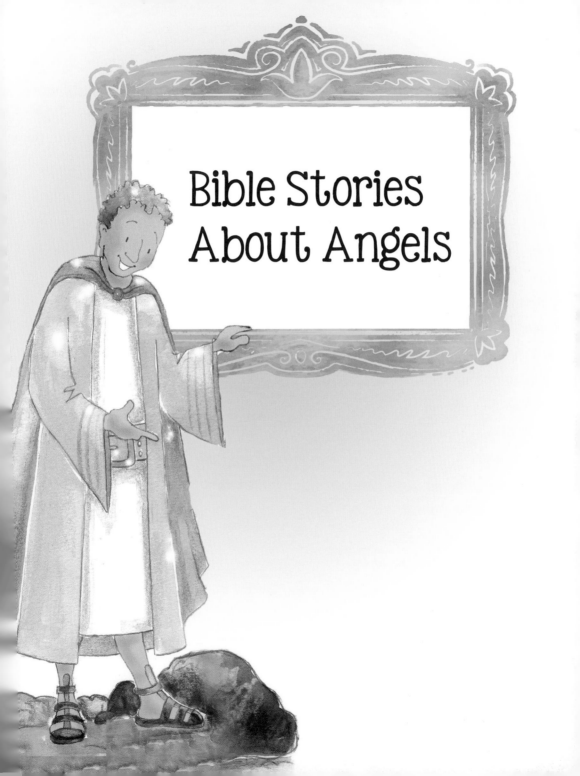

Bible Stories About Angels

God's Little Ones and Their Angels

Matthew 18:10-14

"Beware that you don't look down on any of these little ones. For I tell you that in heaven their angels are always in the presence of my Heavenly Father."

Matthew 18:10

In the Bible, Jesus tells the people not to be cruel to His little ones, because their angels are with God in heaven.

To help the people understand this, Jesus tells them to imagine a farmer with 100 sheep. One day, one of his sheep goes missing. What do you think the farmer did? He left the 99 sheep to go look for the one that got lost. He was so happy when he finally found the lost sheep. In fact, finding the one lost sheep made him even happier than the 99 sheep that never got lost.

Did you know that God is like this farmer? If you get lost and start to do wrong things, God will look for you and help you to stop doing wrong things. He will forgive you for the wrong things you do.

No matter what happens, God and His angels will always look out for you. If you get lost, they will look for you until they find you. If you stumble, they will pick you up and carry you.

An Angel Visits Abraham

Genesis 18:1-15

Be sure to welcome strangers into your home.
By doing this, some people have welcomed
angels as guests, without even knowing it.

Hebrews 13:2 CEV

We have to do our best to always be nice to other people. You never know, one of them might just be an angel or even the Lord Himself.

This is exactly what happened to Abraham. One very warm day he was sitting in front of his tent. Suddenly three visitors appeared close by. Abraham jumped up and bowed his head towards them. He said, "Please come to my home. I am so happy that you have chosen to visit me. I will bring you some water to wash your feet. And let me get you something to eat before you leave."

The visitors answered, "Thank you. We will stay for a little while."

Abraham asked his wife, Sarah, to bake bread for the visitors, using only the best flour she had.

Then he asked one of his servants to cook the best meat they had for the visitors. He did his best to make the visitors feel welcome.

In the end, one of the visitors turned out to be God who had come to give Abraham a very special message – Abraham and his wife would soon have a son!

Imagine how awful it would have been if
Abraham had been unfriendly. We should always
be friendly with everyone no matter who they are.

The Angels in Jacob's Dream

Genesis 28:10-22

In a dream he saw a ladder that reached from earth to heaven, and God's angels were going up and down on it.

Genesis 28:12 CEV

Jacob was on his way to a place called Haran. It was a long journey and he was very tired. When it got dark, Jacob decided to sleep in the field. He looked around for a flat rock and used it as his pillow. Before long, Jacob fell fast asleep.

Jacob dreamed of a very long ladder. The ladder reached all the way to heaven. Angels were climbing up and down the ladder. God was standing next to the ladder. He said: "Jacob, I am the Lord. I will give the land you are sleeping on to you and your family one day. You will have such a big family that they will be like dust on the earth. Wherever they go, things will go well for them. I will always be with you. I will protect you, and give you food

and clothes. I will bring you back here one day. I won't leave you alone. I will do everything that I have promised you."

Jacob woke up and looked around amazed. "This is a very special place," he said. "The Lord is here and I didn't even know it. This must be the ladder to heaven!"

When the sun came up, Jacob took the rock he had used for a pillow and set it upright. He poured oil over the rock and said, "This is the place where I saw God and His angels." He named the place Bethel, which means house of God.

God appeared to Jacob in a dream, showing him angels going up and down a ladder. God wanted Jacob to know that he was not alone - God and His angels would always be with him and take care of him. God and His angels will also be with you whenever you need them.

Hagar and Her Son Are Saved by an Angel

Genesis 21:9-21

The angel of God called to Hagar from heaven and said, "Hagar, what's wrong? Don't be afraid! God has heared the boy crying as he lies there. Go to him and comfort him, for I will make a great nation from his descendants."

Genesis 21:17-18

Sarah was jealous of Hagar and her son, Ishmael. So she told her husband, Abraham, to send them away.

Abraham was very sad. Ishmael was his son and he loved him very much. He didn't want to send them away. But then God told Abraham, "Do not be sad. Do what Sarah told you to do. I will take care of Hagar and Ishmael. I will make him the father of a great nation."

The next morning, Abraham packed a bag with food and filled a leather bag with water for Hagar and Ishmael. Then he sent them away. Hagar did not know where to go. She wandered the desert with Ishmael. When they had drank the last drop of water, she put Ishmael down under a bush.

She felt like they were all alone in the world. She walked away and sat down. She did not want to watch her son die.

Suddenly an angel spoke to her: "What's wrong, Hagar? Don't be afraid. Ishmael will not die. God heard the boy crying. Go, pick up the boy and comfort him. God will give him a lot of children and grandchildren one day."

Hagar immediately did what the angel had told her to do.

Then God showed her a well of water. She filled the leather bag with water and gave Ishmael some water to drink.

From that day on, God was always with Ishmael. Ishmael grew up and stayed in the desert. Everyone talked about what a good hunter he was.

God sent an angel to comfort Hagar when she thought
that her son was going to die. The angel told Hagar
that God would take care of Ishmael and that's exactly
what happened. God will always take care of you, too.

The Angel Who Flew Over Egypt

Exodus 7:14-12:30

The LORD will pass through the land to strike down
the Egyptians. But when He sees the blood on
the doorframe, the LORD will pass over your home.
He will not permit His angel to enter your house.

Exodus 12:23

For a very long time, God's people were slaves of the cruel king of Egypt. One day God decided that enough was enough. He would force the evil king to let His people go. To do this, God sent 10 plagues. The first 9 were:

1. The water was turned into blood
2. A lot of frogs descended on the land and were all over the place
3. Hoards of gnats that bit the people and animals
4. A swarm of flies that were everywhere
5. A sickness that killed all the camels, cows and sheep
6. A disease that covered the Egyptians' bodies in sores
7. Hail storms that destroyed everything
8. Locusts that ate all the plants
9. Complete darkness for three days.

By this time the Egyptians couldn't wait for God's people to leave. But the evil king still refused to let them go, so God told Moses that He would send one last plague.

God gave special instructions to His people before He sent the final plague. He told them to prepare their meal of lamb in a special way for them to eat that night. After they had eaten, they had to smear some of the lamb's blood on the doorframes of their houses. This would keep them safe from the final plague.

God's people did exactly what He had told them to do. After they were all safe and sound inside their houses, God sent His angel to fly over Egypt. The angel took the eldest child of every Egyptian family, even the eldest child of the evil king. When the angel saw a doorframe with blood on it, he knew that God's people were staying there and flew right past. None of God's people got hurt.

Before the sun came up the next morning, the evil king told God's people to leave Egypt immediately. God's people were finally free! They packed their bags and began the long journey home.

Even though God sent 10 plagues, not one of God's people got hurt. With the final plague, God also gave His people special instructions to protect them. Because of this, God's angel did not go near any of God's people. God will always keep us safe when we are obedient to Him.

An Angel Scares Balaam's Donkey

Numbers 22:21-35

God was angry that Balaam was going, so He sent the
angel of the LORD to stand in the road to block his way.

Numbers 22:22

The king of Moab wanted Balaam to come and visit him. Every time he sent his officials to fetch Balaam, Balaam told them to wait until he could ask God about it. God did not want Balaam to go because He knew that the king was up to no good. But the king kept sending officials to Balaam and Balaam kept asking God to let him go. Finally, God told Balaam that he could go as long as he did exactly what God told him to do.

The next morning, Balaam saddled up his donkey and left for Moab. But God was not too happy with the way Balaam had behaved. So God sent an angel to stand in the middle of the road to stop him. The donkey got such a fright when he saw the angel in the road that it left the road and ran into the open field. Balaam got angry and beat the donkey.

Once back on the road, the road got to be very narrow with a stone wall on either side. Again the angel appeared in the middle of the road. There was nowhere for the donkey to run this time. He tried to pass between the angel and the wall, but scraped Balaam's foot against the wall. Balaam got angry again and beat the poor donkey a second time.

For a while they walked on without any problems, but then the angel appeared again. This time the road was too narrow for the donkey to pass the angel, so the donkey just lay down. Balaam got very angry this time. He grabbed a stick to beat the donkey again. Suddenly, God made the donkey speak. The donkey asked Balaam, "What did I do to make you beat me three times?"

"You made me look stupid!" shouted Balaam. "Be thankful I don't have a sword!"

So the donkey asked, "Have I ever let you down?"

"No," Balaam admitted.

At that moment, God opened Balaam's eyes so that he could also see the angel. Balaam got a big fright. He bowed down low before the angel.

"Why did you beat your poor donkey three times?" the angel asked angrily. "If the donkey hadn't stopped those three times, I would have killed you by now! I would have just spared the life of the obedient donkey!"

Then Balaam told the angel, "I was wrong. I did not know that you were trying to stop me. I will turn back if God doesn't want me to go."

The angel of God replied, "No, you can go. But remember to only do what God tells you to do."

When Balaam first asked God to go, he did not listen when God said no. Balaam kept asking and God kept saying no. In the end, God told Balaam he could go, but He was not happy about how Balaam had behaved. That is why God sent the angel to teach Balaam a lesson. We must always listen to God. He knows what's best for us and will never give us bad advice.

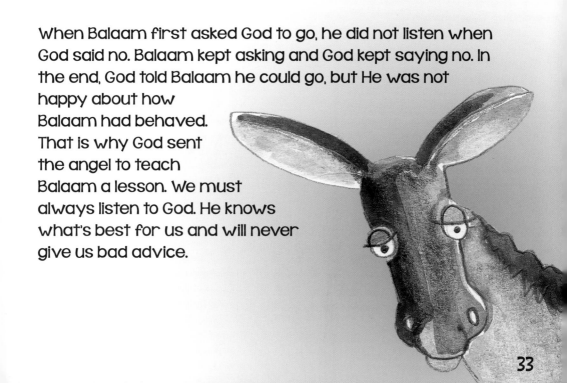

An Angel Feeds Elijah

1 Kings 19:1-8

An angel woke him up and said, "Get up and eat." Elijah looked around, and by his head was a jar of water and some baked bread.

1 Kings 19:5-6 CEV

The prophet Elijah was in big trouble. King Ahab's wife was very angry with him, because he had killed all the prophets of Baal. So she sent him an angry message promising to have him killed before the end of the following day.

Elijah was very scared. All he could do was to flee to the desert. He walked in the hot sun all day. Finally he stopped, too tired to go any further. Elijah sat down under a tree to rest. "I have had enough, Lord," he said. "Rather let me die."

Tired, Elijah fell asleep. Suddenly an angel woke Elijah up and said, "Get up and eat!"

He looked around and, to his surprise, found a loaf of bread and a jug of water standing nearby. He ate and drank, and lay down again. But the angel woke him up again and said, "Get up and eat some more! You need all the energy you can get for the long journey ahead of you."

Elijah did as he was told. He ate all of the bread and drank all of the water. He now

34

had enough energy to walk for 40 days and nights to Mount Horeb where he hid in a cave.

When Elijah asked God for help, God sent His angel to help him. God will do the same for you. All you have to do is tell God what you need. God listens when we pray and He will help you.

An Angel Saves Daniel from the Lions

Daniel 6:1-28

"God sent His angel to shut the lions' mouths so that they
would not hurt me, for I have been found innocent in His sight."

Daniel 6:22

Daniel loved God and was always obedient. He prayed three times a day.

Some people were jealous of Daniel because the king liked him so much. So they came up with a very nasty plan.

They went to the king and said, "Your majesty, it's time that the people show you how much they like you. For thirty days all the people must only pray to you. Anyone who refuses must be thrown into the lions' den!"

The law was written down and the king signed it to make sure that no one could ever change it.

Daniel heard about the new law, but he loved God and didn't want to stop praying to Him. So Daniel kept praying to God three times a day.

The people who had come up with the nasty plan saw Daniel pray and immediately ran to tell the king.

"Did you not make it a law that everyone must pray to you and to no one else?" they asked the king. "Yes, I did," he answered.

"Did you not say that everyone who does not obey this law must be thrown into the lions' den?" they asked the king again.

"Yes, I did," answered the king.

"Well, Daniel broke the law!" they said very impressed with themselves.

The king was very upset. The rest of the day he tried to think of a way to save Daniel's life. But it was too late. Not even the king could change the law once it had been written down and signed.

The king had no choice but to send his soldiers to capture Daniel. Before they threw him into the lions' den, the king said to Daniel: "May the God you pray to save you."

To make sure that no one could let Daniel out of the lions' den, the soldiers placed a big stone in front of the entrance.

That night the king did not sleep at all. He was thinking about his friend Daniel. Very early the next morning the king went to the lions' den to check on him.

"Daniel!" he shouted nervously. "Did your God keep you safe?"

Daniel cheerfully answered, "My God knows that I have done nothing wrong. So He sent His angel to keep the lions from eating me."

The king was so happy. He called his soldiers to help Daniel out of the lions' den. Then he ordered them to capture the people who had tricked him into signing the law. They were to be thrown into the lions' den. The king wanted everyone to know what God had done for Daniel. He wrote a letter and sent his messengers to tell everyone this: "I command everyone in my kingdom to pray to Daniel's God. He rescues people and sets them free. He performs great miracles in heaven and on earth. He saved Daniel from the lions."

Daniel was very happy and praised God.

Daniel knew that praying to the king would be wrong. This would be like worshiping an idol. We are only to pray to God. Daniel knew this and chose to obey God. Because of this, God sent His angel to protect Daniel. No matter what people say, you should never do anything you know that God wouldn't like.

Daniel Sees an Angel

Daniel 9-10

The angel touched me and said, "Don't be frightened! God thinks highly of you, and He intends this for your good, so be brave and strong." At this, I regained my strength and replied, "Please speak! You have already made me feel much better."

Daniel 10:18-19 CEV

God's people had done many wrong things and had not listened to God. Daniel knew that if they did not make things right, God would destroy their city. Daniel was scared. He asked God to forgive all of the people and to not destroy the city.

Before Daniel had even finished praying, the angel Gabriel came and told Daniel: "Don't be afraid. God has heard your prayer and sent me to give you a message. The people have done many wrong things. If God doesn't do something, they will not stop."

The angel explained to Daniel that a big war would break out. The people would go through a very tough time. But, when the time was right, God would destroy the enemy and rescue His people.

This message upset Daniel so much that he could barely eat or drink anything for three weeks. Then God sent another angel.

The angel said to Daniel, "Don't be afraid. God heard your prayer and has sent me to help you understand His message."

Daniel said to the angel, "God's message made me very upset. I have lost all of my strength. How can I talk to someone as powerful as you when I am so weak?"

The angel stretched out his hand and touched Daniel's lips. Daniel could feel his strength coming back. Then the angel said to him, "Don't be afraid. God will make sure that everything works out the way that it should. Take courage and be strong. God will be with you."

God's first message really scared Daniel, so
God sent another angel to comfort him and to
give him strength. If you ever feel scared, ask God
to help you. He will give you strength and help you.

Gabriel Brings Zechariah Good News

Luke 1:8-25, 57-65

The angel said, "I am Gabriel! I stand in the very presence of God. It was He who sent me to bring you this good news!"

Luke 1:19

Zechariah and his wife, Elizabeth, were very old. They had no children. For a long time they prayed, asking God to give them a baby, but nothing happened.

One day Zechariah was busy working in the temple. His job was to go into the temple and burn the incense. Suddenly an angel appeared in the temple where he was working. Zechariah got a big fright.

The angel said to him, "Don't be afraid, Zechariah. God has heard your prayers. Elizabeth will have a son. You must name him John. He will be a great servant of the Lord. He will lead people back to God. He will get the people ready for the Lord."

Zechariah could not believe it. "How can I be sure that this will happen? My wife and I are very old," he said.

Then the angel told him, "My name is Gabriel. I work for God. He has sent me with this good news. But because you refuse to believe what I have told you, you will not be able to speak one word until your son is born. You'll see, everything will happen exactly as I have said."

Zechariah finished his work and went home. His voice was completely gone; he could not speak one word.

Shortly afterwards Elizabeth became pregnant. She was very happy and said, "The Lord has done something wonderful for me."

Zechariah and Elizabeth's friends and family were glad when their baby boy was born. Everyone wanted the little one to be named after his father, Zechariah.

"No, his name is John," said Elizabeth.

"But, why?" they wanted to know. "There is no one in your family with the name John."

"Let's ask Zechariah what he thinks," someone suggested.

Zechariah, who had been listening, gestured with a smile for them to bring a piece of paper and something to write with. He wrote, "His name is John."

Everyone was very surprised. They didn't know what to say.

At that moment, Zechariah got his voice back. After more than nine months, he was able to speak again. Zechariah started praising God right away.

God did not immediately answer Zechariah and his wife's prayers for a child. Only when they were very old did God give them a child. When we pray, God doesn't always answer us right away. He has perfect timing and will answer our prayers when the time is right.

Mary Gets Good News from Gabriel

Luke 1:26-36

The angel told Mary, "Don't be afraid! God is pleased with you, and you will have a Son. His name will be Jesus. He will be great and will be called the Son of God."

Luke 1:30-32 CEV

While Elizabeth was pregnant with John, God sent an angel to Nazareth. His name was Gabriel. He had to deliver a very important message to a girl named Mary. She was engaged to be married to a very good man, Joseph.

The angel greeted Mary and said, "You are truly blessed! God is with you!"

Mary did not understand what Gabriel was trying to tell her. He explained: "Don't be afraid. God has a wonderful surprise for you. You will soon have a Son. His name will be Jesus. He will be very great. He will be called the Son of God. God will make Him King over all of His people. He will be King forever."

Mary asked Gabriel, "How is that possible? I'm not even married yet."

"God will give you this Baby. Look at your relative Elizabeth. Nobody thought she would ever have a child. But in three months' time she will have a son, even though she is so old. Nothing is impossible for God."

Mary said, "I belong to God. Let everything happen exactly as you have said."

God sent Gabriel to bring Mary the good news that she would have a Child. This news was the best news Gabriel had ever delivered. This was the beginning of Jesus' journey on earth. Soon Jesus would be born and He would save us all!

An Angel Visits Joseph in a Dream

Matthew 1:18-24

While Joseph was thinking about this, an angel from the
Lord came to him in a dream. The angel said, "Joseph,
the baby that Mary will have is from the Holy Spirit."

Matthew 1:20 CEV

Mary was very excited about having a baby. But Joseph, her fiancé, was worried. In those days it was unacceptable for a woman who is not married to have a baby. Joseph didn't want the people to gossip about him or Mary. He made plans to secretly break off the engagement.

One night, while Joseph was still trying to make his mind up about what to do, he had a dream. An angel appeared to him in the dream and said, "Joseph, you must marry Mary. Don't worry about anything. The Holy Spirit gave Mary her Baby. Soon she will have a Baby Boy. You must name Him Jesus. He will save the people from their sins."

When Joseph woke up, he did exactly what the angel had told him to do and married Mary.

If God asks us to do something,
we should do it no matter
how scared we are or what
other people might say.
Trust that God has a plan.

The Shepherds Are Visited by Angels

Luke 2:8-20

Suddenly, an angel of the Lord appeared among them ... "Don't be afraid!" he said. "I bring you good news. The Savior – yes, the Messiah, the Lord – has been born today in Bethlehem! And you will recognize Him by this sign: You will find a Baby wrapped snugly in strips of cloth, lying in a manger."

Luke 2:9-12

Just outside of Bethlehem, a group of shepherds were looking after their sheep in a field. Suddenly, an angel appeared to them. The shepherds were frightened, but the angel said, "Don't be afraid. I have good news that will make you and everyone in the world very happy. Today a Savior has been born. He will save you from your sins. He is the Messiah. Go see for yourselves! You will find a Baby wrapped up in cloth, lying in a manger. That is Him!"

The next moment the shepherds saw many angels coming down from heaven. They joined the angel who had been talking to them.

There in the field underneath the stars the angels started to sing. Never before had the shepherds heard such beautiful music.

The angels sang, "Praise God. Praise our Father in heaven. And peace on earth to everyone who pleases Him."

After the angels had finished singing, they went back to heaven. The shepherds hurried off to Bethlehem. There they found Joseph and Mary, and Baby Jesus lying in a manger. They told Mary and Joseph what the angel had said. Mary kept their words in her heart and thought of them often.

Later the shepherds returned to their sheep. They were very happy, and praised God for all they had seen and heard.

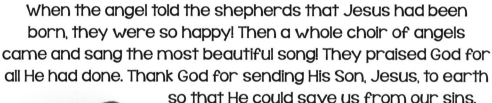

When the angel told the shepherds that Jesus had been born, they were so happy! Then a whole choir of angels came and sang the most beautiful song! They praised God for all He had done. Thank God for sending His Son, Jesus, to earth so that He could save us from our sins.

An Angel Warns Joseph

Matthew 2:13-23

"Get up! Flee to Egypt with the child and His mother," the
angel said. "Stay there until I tell you to return, because
Herod is going to search for the child to kill Him."

Matthew 2:13

Not everyone was happy about Jesus' birth. King Herod was jealous. He did not want anyone else to take his place as king, especially not a Baby called the Son of God. So he came up with an evil plan to track Jesus down and kill Him.

An angel of the Lord appeared to Joseph in a dream. "Wake up!" he said. "Take Jesus and His mother and flee to Egypt. Stay there until you hear from me again. King Herod is looking for Jesus. He wants to kill Him."

Joseph immediately got up. It was still dark outside. He woke Mary and packed their things. They quietly left and went to Egypt just like the angel had told them to.

After the evil King Herod had died, the angel appeared to Joseph in another dream. "Wake up!" he said. "Take Jesus and His mother back to Israel. Everyone who wanted to kill Him, has died."

Again Joseph did exactly what the angel had told him to do. Joseph, Mary and Jesus went all the way back to Israel. They stayed in a town called Nazareth. They were finally safe.

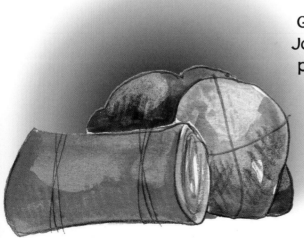

God sent an angel to warn Joseph about King Herod's evil plan. God is always with us. He looks out for us and protects us. With Him by our side, we've got nothing to fear.

The Angels Take Care of Jesus

Matthew 4:1-11

Angels came and
took care of Jesus.

Matthew 4:11

After Jesus was baptized, He went into the desert. There He ate nothing for forty days and forty nights. This was the opportunity the devil had been waiting for. When Jesus was very hungry, the devil appeared. He said, "If You really are the Son of God, then You can turn these stones into bread."

But Jesus knew what the devil was planning. He answered, "The Bible teaches us that no one can live only on food. People need every word that God has spoken."

The devil didn't like this one bit. He took Jesus to the highest point of the temple in Jerusalem. Then he said to Jesus, "If You really are the Son of God, You can jump off this roof and not get hurt. The Bible says that God's angels will protect You. They will carry You so that You won't even stub Your toe against a rock."

But Jesus had an answer ready. He said, "Yes, but the Bible also says that we must not test God or mock Him."

The devil decided to try one last time. He took Jesus to a very high mountain. There he showed Jesus all the kingdoms on earth and their power. He said, "I will give all of this to You if You bow down and worship me."

But Jesus had had enough of the devil's tricks. "Go away, Satan!" He said. "The Bible teaches us to worship God and only Him."

Then the devil left. Jesus was left alone in the desert. He was very tired, hungry and thirsty. So God sent His angels to take care of Jesus. They made sure that Jesus got everything He needed!

The devil tried to trick Jesus into turning against God. Even though Jesus was very tired, hungry and thirsty, He did not listen to the devil. After the devil had left, God sent His angels to take care of Jesus. No matter what happens, God will always take care of His children!

The Angel at Jesus' Grave

Matthew 28:1-10

An angel of the Lord came down from heaven, rolled aside the stone, and sat on it. "Don't be afraid!" he said. "I know you are looking for Jesus, who was crucified. He isn't here! He is risen from the dead, just as He said would happen."

Matthew 28:2, 5-6

Three days after Jesus' death, two women went to visit His grave. Suddenly a strong earthquake struck. An angel came down from heaven. The angel's face shone like lightning and his clothes were as white as snow. He rolled away the stone in front of Jesus' grave and sat on it.

The guards watching Jesus' grave shook with fear and fainted. But the angel gently said to the women, "Don't be afraid! I know you are looking for Jesus, who was crucified. He is not here! Jesus Himself said that He would come back to life. And that is exactly what has happened."

Then the angel pointed to the place where Jesus' body used to be. "See for yourselves. Now, hurry! Go tell His disciples what has happened. Tell them that He is on His way to Galilee. You will find Him there."

The women did not waste any time. On their way back though, they met Jesus Himself. Oh how wonderful it was to see Him again! Just like the angel had done, Jesus told them to tell His disciples that He was alive and would meet them in Galilee. And that's exactly what they did.

God sent His angel to remind the disciples that, before His death, Jesus had told them that He would rise from the dead. God wanted them to understand and know what this meant. When Jesus died on the cross, He died for our sins. When He came back to life again, He overcame death and the sin that goes with it. Because of this, those who believe in Jesus will one day be able to live with Him in heaven.

An Angel Sends Philip on a Mission

Acts 8:26-39

> The Lord's angel said to Philip,
> "Go south along the desert road
> that leads from Jerusalem to Gaza."
>
> Acts 8:26 CEV

Philip believed in God and told others the good news about what Jesus had done for us. One day God sent an angel to give Philip a message. The angel said, "Philip, take the quiet road from Jerusalem to Gaza. Remember to walk south all the way."

Philip wondered why he had to take that specific road. But he knew that there would be a good reason for it. He packed his bag and left.

On the road Philip saw an important Ethiopian official in a carriage. The man worked for the queen of Ethiopia and was on his way home.

God's Spirit told Philip to catch up to the man. As he got closer, Philip heard the man reading from the book of Isaiah. "Excuse me, sir. Do you understand what you are reading?" Philip asked.

"No," sighed the man. "There is no one who can explain it to me."

The man invited Philip to ride with him in his carriage. He then read the passage that he didn't understand to Philip: "He was led like a sheep on its way to be killed. He was silent as a lamb whose wool is being cut off, and He did not say a word. He was treated like a nobody and did not receive a fair trial. How can He have children, if His life is snatched away?" (Acts 8:32-33 CEV)

"Who is Isaiah talking about?" the man wanted to know.

Philip then told him about Jesus. He told him that Isaiah had predicted a long time ago how Jesus would die on the cross for the sins of the whole world. He also told him that Jesus had risen from the dead, and that everyone who believes in Jesus, will be saved.

As they were traveling, they passed by a place where there was some water. The man stopped the carriage and asked Philip to baptize him. Being baptized means that you believe the good news about Jesus and that you are now a child of God. After Philip had baptized the man, God's Spirit came and took Philip away. The man never saw Philip again, but he was very happy as he got back in his carriage and continued home.

The angel told Philip to walk down a specific road. Even though he did not know why, he knew that God would have a good reason for asking him to do it. If Philip hadn't gone, the Ethiopian man would never have become a child of God. Trust that God has a special plan for you too. You might not always know what it is, but know that God always has a good reason for everything He does.

An Angel Rescues Peter

Acts 12:1-11

Suddenly, there was a bright light in the cell, and
an angel of the Lord stood before Peter. The angel
struck him on the side to awaken him and said,
"Quick! Get up!" And the chains fell off his wrists.

Acts 12:7

Peter was arrested and thrown in jail because he believed in God. When the other believers heard about this, they all started to pray for him.

The day before Peter had to stand trial, King Herod had him bound with two chains and ordered two soldiers, one on either side of Peter, to guard him. More soldiers guarded the prison gate. There was no way Peter could escape.

Suddenly an angel of the Lord appeared in Peter's cell. A bright light shone around him. Peter was fast asleep and didn't realize what was going on. "Get up!" said the angel as he woke Peter. At that moment Peter's chains fell off.

"Get dressed and put on your sandals," said the angel.

After Peter had dressed, the angel told him, "Put on your coat and follow me."

Peter was sure that he was dreaming. But no, they were walking past all the guards!

Before he knew it, they were standing in front of the prison gate. The gate opened by itself. Peter and the angel walked out together.

Then the angel suddenly disappeared. Peter was very excited. He could hear his heart beating in his chest. "The Lord really sent an angel to rescue me!" he said amazed.

Even though Peter had done nothing wrong, he was thrown in jail because he believed in God. God sent an angel to rescue Peter. God knows everything that happens here on earth. If you are in trouble, God already knows about it. He will help you. He will send His angels to protect you (see Psalm 91:11).

Be Like an Angel!

Galatians 5:22-23

God's Spirit makes us loving, happy, peaceful, patient, kind, good, faithful, gentle, and self-controlled. There is no law against behaving in any of these ways.

Galatians 5:22-23 CEV

When you have God's Spirit in your heart, you want to do good things. Almost like a tree that bears good and healthy fruit. Unfortunately, it's not always that easy. Just like a tree can sometimes bear sour and rotten fruit, we too do wrong things. But it is never too late to tell Jesus that you're sorry. He will help you to do your best to only do good things.

Try each day to be a little more like an angel. They are kind, loving, peaceful, patient, good and always listen to God. If we all tried our best to be more like angels, the world would be a better and more beautiful place.

If you haven't already, ask God to help you to be loving, happy, peaceful, patient, kind, good, faithful, gentle, and self-controlled like the angels are.

Create Your Own Pop-up Angel Card

You will need:

- One A4 colored cardboard

- Glue stick

- Ruler
- Pencil
- Scissors

- Paint, coloring pencils or colored felt-tip pens

- Stickers and wrapping paper to decorate with

What to do:

1. Fold the cardboard in half like you would a card. Open the card and cut along the fold. Take one half and fold it in half again like before. Decorate the outer edges of the inside of the card.

2. Use a pencil and ruler to draw a strip of 15cm long x 3cm wide on the other half of the cardboard. Cut it out and fold the strip in half. Make two folds 2cm away from the corners to create two flaps.

3. Glue the two flaps to the card – one on either edge of the card. Make sure that the fold in the card and the fold in the middle of the strip line up.

4. Trace the angel on the next page onto the leftover piece of cardboard. Decorate the angel.

5. Fold the angel lengthwise in half. Glue the angel to the pop-up strip – the fold on the strip and the fold on the angel should line up.

6. Open your card ... and see how your angel pops up!

Other Books by Wendy Maartens

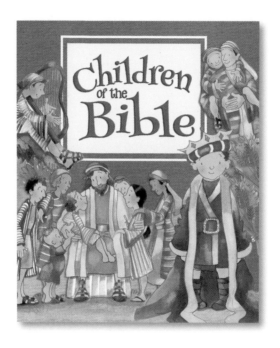

ISBN 978-1-4321-1570-8

God uses ordinary children to do extraordinary things. Discover the special plan God had for the ordinary children in the Bible with these 19 adventure-filled stories from the Old and New Testaments. Just like God had a special plan for them, He also has a special plan for you!

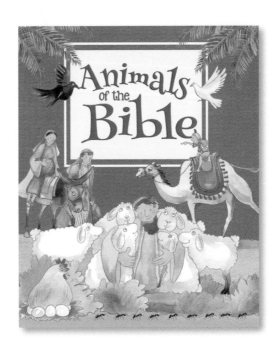

ISBN 978-1-4321-1699-6

In 30 Old and New Testament stories, *Animals of the Bible* will teach kids all about God's wonderful creatures! They will have fun uncovering all sorts of interesting facts about the animals, like why lizards sometimes lose their tails or donkeys have such big ears. Eager beavers will also learn some super sayings inspired by these animals. In two shakes of a lamb's tail they'll learn all about the animals in the Bible!